ONCE UPON
A
PRETTY PENCIL

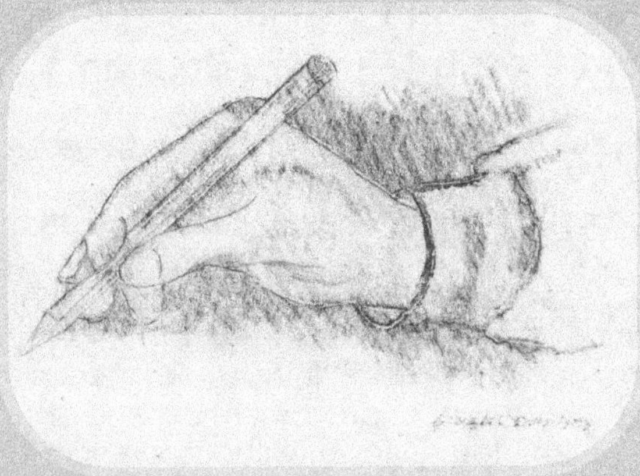

I WROTE SOME WORDS SO DEAR

MY MEMORY'S NOT LONG

THE WORDS ARE GONE

BUT THE THOUGHTS

ARE ALL IN

HERE

By

Richard Zuspan

<u>Acknowledgements</u>

This book is a composite of the art work of Ginger Lovellette and the poetry of Richard Zuspan

Some serious, some whimsical, some inspirational and all from the heart.

Ginger's art talent lies mostly in the area of abstract, expressionism and she also does beautiful landscapes. She has a way of expressing herself with a paint brush, palette knife and even with pieces of paper.

I love the strict structural demands of poetry. The challenge of getting across the message you are stressing; while maintaining the rhyme or meter or even shape of your structural confines, is a challenge. But when successful, the message is driven home.

Thanks also to my high school friend, Rex Krueger for his editorial expertise, without which this book could never have been produced.

A tribute to Ginger
My muse, My inspiration

You make my heart go pity-pat the way it was at first.

After all these birthdays past, even makes it seem to burst.

The years just get better as our life goes on its way.

Each year sees new ways to go and shows us where to

stay.

Each birthday is a mile-stone; not of age,

but a marking of joy for us and the setting of a new stage.

Table of Contents

Table of Contents (cont.)

Table of Contents (cont.)

God, Man and Satan

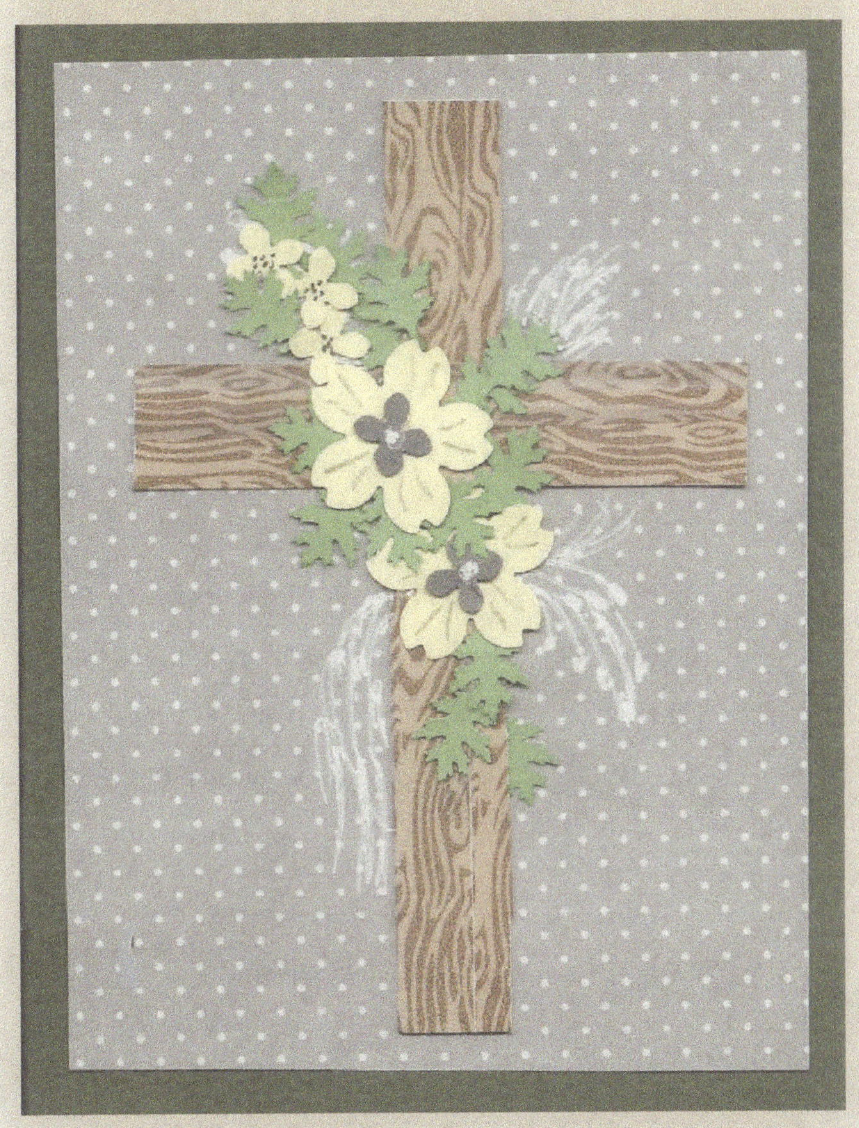

The Only Path To Heaven

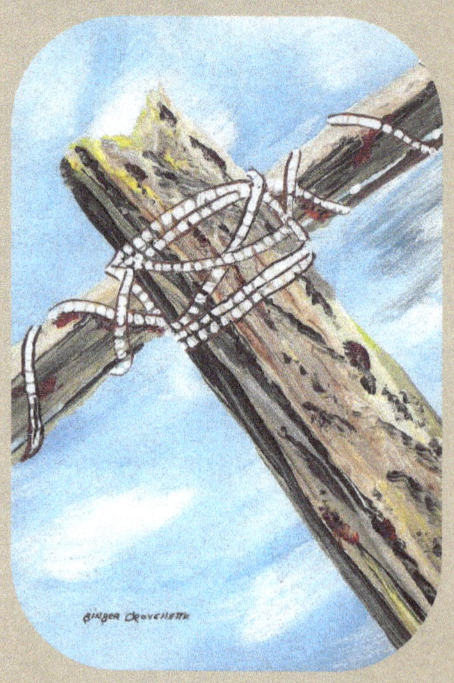

Having begun in spirit, are you now made perfect by the flesh?

Only One can make you perfect and only at your request.

Only through His suffering can you be made whole.

Only through His love will you save your soul.

Look up to the cross to feel the crucifixion.

Then pray thanks for your redemption.

He returns your love with certainty.

That's the path to eternity.

God's Indomitable Power Shown In The Beauty Of A Flower

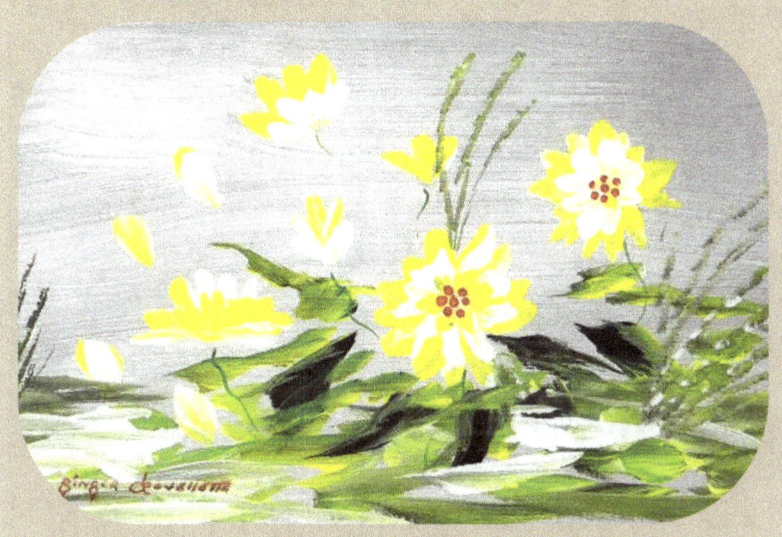

The glory of a blossoming flower

exemplifies Gods endless power.

The boundless gifts of His creation

are given without consideration.

The beauty of flowers is but one gift bestowed

upon a world from which much is owed.

Due to the unequaled and revered one,

His crucified and sin forgiving Son.

God Is Love

Our God is not a harsh God.
All He wants is love and obedience.
So grace this earth that we trod
and fear not to seek repentance.

Love your neighbor as yourself
and live life with good sense.
Don't obsess and strive for wealth
or advance yourself at others expense.

His rules are simple and written in a book.
Read it often for great guidance.
That will give you the best outlook.
It will keep you in compliance.

There is this enemy in your way,
He tries to change your thinking.
Satan nudges you every day
and creates new ways of sinning.

So read the book and say your prayers.
And ask Him for help and protection
He will relieve you of your cares
and will stand by you without exception.

<u>Satan Wants You</u>

I hear him knocking on my door

Tap, tap, tapping softly but more and more.

Everywhere I hear his voice or see his face

cooing, whispering, tempting grace.

"Don't you wish you had his riches."

"Or: You can live like those oil prince's."

"Be brave and take a chance

You can win it all on that dance".

Satan loves to take you down and make

you think you've won the round.

When all along you sink deeper, descending closer

to your fear.

He loves to lure you to the sin. Then laugh as it

sucks you in.

Don't fall for his wily ways that make you think

you rule your days.

Look only to Jesus for salvation. Through Him

you fight temptation.

Ask God to give your life peace. He will help

you fight that beast.

<u>We All Are</u>
<u>The Product Of Our Decisions</u>

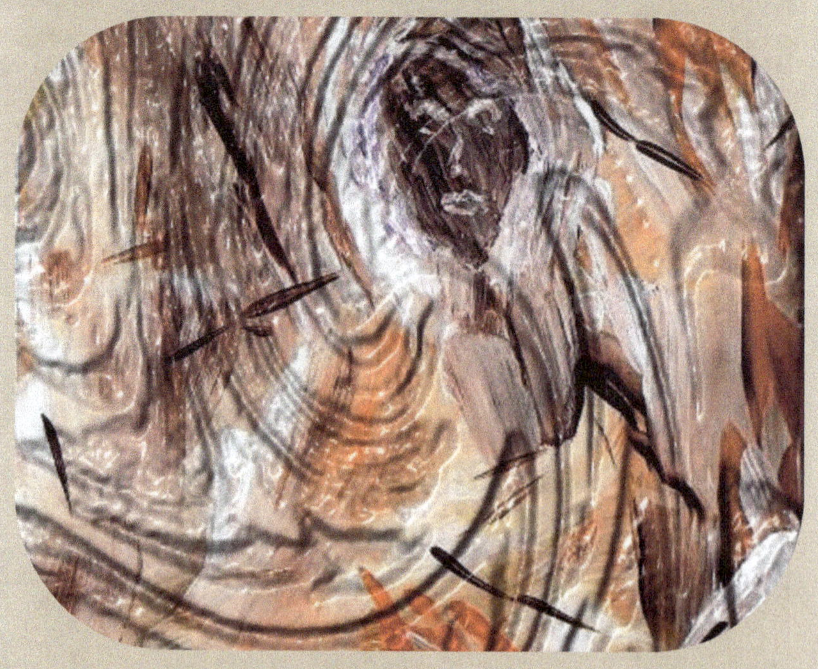

You may be the <u>bride of the evil</u> one himself

or perhaps you are the sum total of evil its self.

For all of your long gone beauty and charm

you look as one who can do no more harm.

Wallow in your self earned misery

and think of what your pleasure could be.

You once were promised love for eternity.

But turned your back on Calvary.

<u>Walk With Jesus</u>

Draw your swords,
menace my wife.
Hammer me with words
and threaten my life.
But we walk with Jesus
and your acts do not deceive us.

Though Satan shows his evil ways,
we will love our Lord all our days.
Our desire is to walk in righteousness
and show Christian mindfulness.
Because we walk with Jesus
nothing can distress us.

There is a fork in every road
and that's where Satan lays his load.
He'll make you think that left is right,
then suddenly he'll blur your sight.
But since we walk with Jesus
nothing will distract us.

Not money not power nor Hollywood status.
can compare to the love He has for us.
Cupped in His hands away from the wind
His protection is everlasting. It does not end.
When we walk with Jesus
Nothing can harm us.

Proof of God Is Everywhere

I see His foot prints everywhere,
from the snowy mountains to clouds in the air.
Even bustling busy city streets,
and quiet rural retreats.

Besides being recipients of unending love,
we are blessed by such beauty from above.
Our God offers His opportunity
to gain peace and tranquility.

Trust in the Lord and believe in His Son
and your life eternal with Him is won.
I see His foot prints everywhere
even though I am often unaware.

He has marked my heart and altered my goal.
Not status, money or fame will buy my soul.
His promise of eternal life
unmarked by pain, woe or strife,

Makes me realize no calamity on this earth
defeats the promise of heavens new birth.
I walk in His path and follow His lead
hoping others will take heed.

God's Chart for Columbus

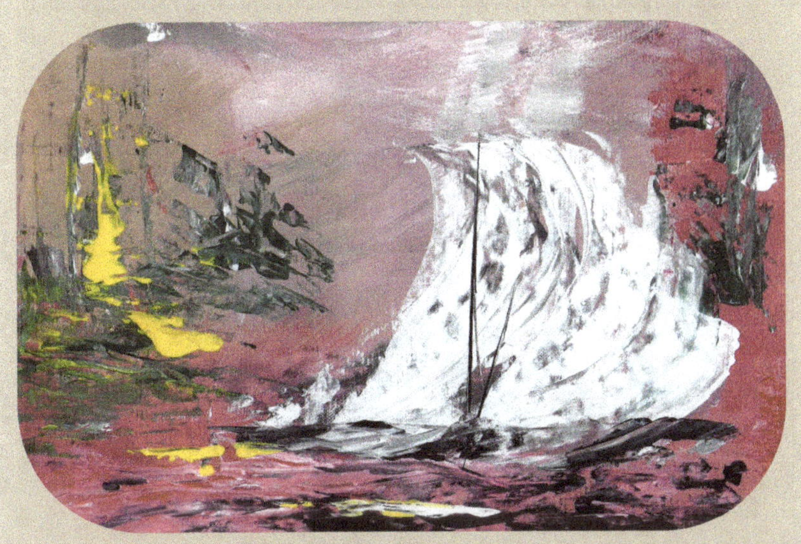

Released; he
sailed to find the East.
But God lead them to a West,
that turned out for us to be the best.
Did He not have in mind a promised land?
A providential nation where worshipers could stand.
Living by His rules and loving Him as He Loves us.
To obey His Christ's teachings and ignoring lust.
Helping each other to an easier and better day.
Following the path He did originally lay.
And protecting his beloved chosen,
from those Satan set in motion.
We must return humbly
and seek humility,
or it's good day
to our USA.

Satan Knows Your Weakness

Satan knows your weakness,
he strives for your demise.
He will promise fame and glory,
then award you **his** prize.

Never wonder what it is that Satan has to offer.
He will make you think it's riches
then lead you to the slaughter.

He will make you doubt your thinking and ask
"who is Jesus Christ?"
when all along he knew, you'd have to pay the price.

The cost you will have to pay will be a higher toll
than any you expected and never was your goal.

But lusting present gain and the promise of future fame,
takes you out of the grace of Christ and
puts you
in the hall of shame.

Never want beyond your needs
as craving the excess will plant seeds.

When you give a hand to those who lack,
you'll build
a shield against Satan's attack.

But most importantly for your protection
and a shield from satan's damnation;
is the strength from
knowing Jesus Christ,
and
His promise Of salvation.

Raising Children

How difficult the task to raise a child
in this world of huge distractions.
All children will show they are wild
and that makes need of firm actions.

How easy it is to give in to a tantrum
because it's noisy or embarrassing.
It's easier to relent to the hoodlum
than it is to be strong and embracing.

By reflecting the love of Jesus firsthand
And teaching them to trust in Christ
the children will know where they stand.
they'll walk fearlessly the rest of their life

It takes strong character and great inner strength
to limit your children and set boundaries.
And it takes deep seated love to go the full length
loving your children and forgoing your luxuries.

Whether you want it or not; God has laid
upon you a duty.

Get out of yourself and into the children
and develop their inner beauty.

<u>The First Harbinger</u>

(Isaiah Chapter 9)

On this special day we thank our Lord
for that time of grace from the Assyrian sword.
We thank Him that He gave His word
that our prayers would not go unheard.
That if only we'd believe in Him
we would be forgiven of our sin.
We thank Him that He gave His Son
that through Him our eternal life is won.

This is a special time of appreciation
for His hand in founding our nation.
He offered up a new promised land.
A place to worship and follow his command.
A place of no idols or golden hind.
A place where all men are of equal kind.
This new promised land of hope for mankind
set on the precept that no man be maligned
thrived for two centuries
honoring God and His laws.
Sharing <u>our</u> wealth and protection
with only some flaws.

Now we are at a crossroad in time
He lifted His shield
on the eleventh day of month nine.
We had turned our backs and established idols
instead of bowing to him and heeding the Gospels.
Wealth and fame, power and prestige,
for those gods we go to our knees.
The children of Ishmael have crossed our border,
desecrated our buildings and upset our order.
To turn to ourselves and say "we can conquer"
shows our arrogance and need to concur.
Let us once again bow to our Lord
and humbly ask his protection from the sword.

You Are The Master
Of Your Soul

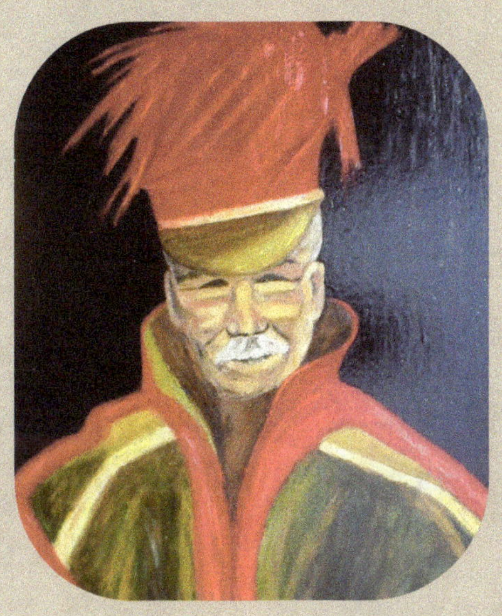

I am the captain of my life and
commander of my soul.
The vessel that I steer is headed for heaven;
that's my goal.

My Savior has anointed me with
the oil of forgiveness.
And all He asks is we reflect His love and
be His witness.

Believe in Him and
He will be in our heart.
Trust in Him and
we will never be apart.

Black Eyed Dog

Cuddly dog with black black eyes
Helps to make you realize.
This cute little animal is your friend
And upon you he wants to depend.
Being kind to this one shows your character
And earns you the right to be his proprietor.
But never forget things are on loan from God
How they are treated is entered into your log.

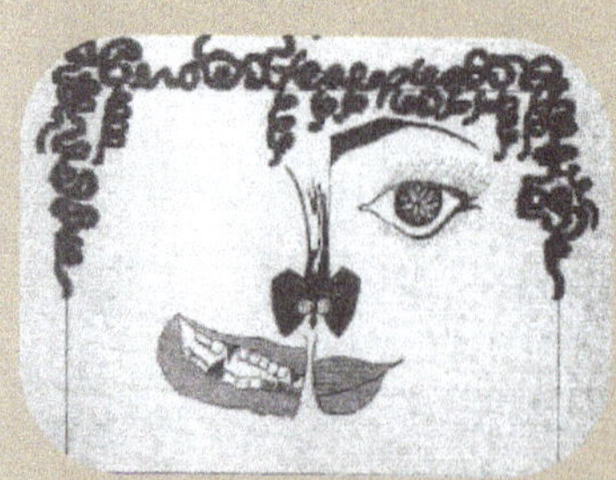

Curly Headed Girl

Curly headed girl so hard to know.
Makes me want to help you show,
how good you really have become
over the years and more than some.
You honestly hoped for personal success
to get you out of this ugly mess.
But since you know God loves you so,
don't forget to pray for his console.

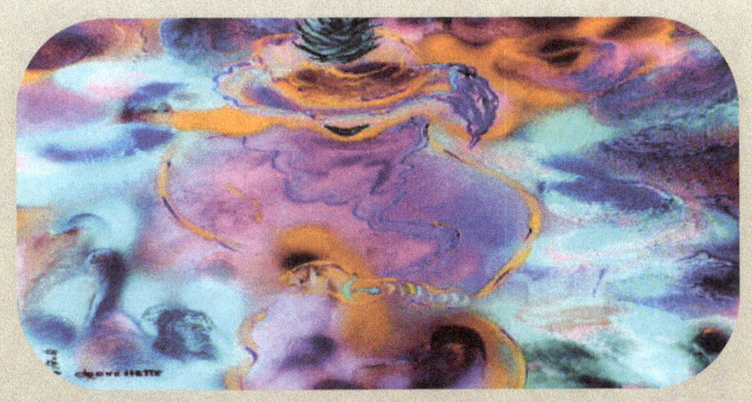

<u>Winning Happiness</u>

Clowns and gorillas all in a haze
Is it my dream or the newest craz?
Looks like they're having fun.
But then again why do they run
Away from this town just to go there,
Then turn around again to go somewhere.
Maybe the clown is the one that is running,
Afraid of that crusader that is soon coming
Behind her on a quest to conquer her soul.
Saving people from Satan wasn't their goal.
Killing and pillaging to convert heathens
To a religion as Christ-less as their own demons.
Jesus asked us to love him and to treat others
In the same manner as you would treat brothers.
Take yourself out of you and put others before.
You will win in the end the happiness you look for. ..

Christ Died On The Cross for the Redemption of All Mankind

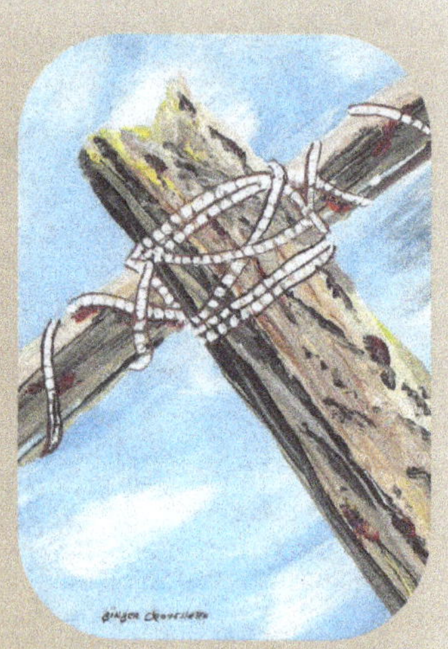

Of all the ways a man can die,
on the cross would be rated
most high.

For our Savior to die in that much pain
shows it's freedom from sin He wants us
to gain.

Don't let Satan cloud your senses
and cover you with evil
pretenses.

Nor tempt you into evil thoughts
leading you to
eternal loss.

Love God with all your heart
and from Jesus
never part.

The Attack Of The Assyrians

The Assyrians have struck smashing your fence.
Yet you look to yourself for your own defense.
Do you not realize the years of protection
I have given for just your affection.

I am your Lord and I provided your protection
because you loved Me and
worshiped without exception.
Then came your modern day idols.
Taking your hearts away from your Bibles.

Chasing money and fame.
Glory, stardom and a big name.
Those were your gods that ruled your life.
Forgetting your God that relieved your strife.

Chasing the thrills of self esteem.
Hoping to win that great dream.
You threw Me out of your schools.
Forbid the reading of My rules.

Adjusted My teachings to allow your sin.
Then adopted new ways to let Satan in.
Humble yourself, face Me and turn from your ways.
Then I will protect you the rest of your days.

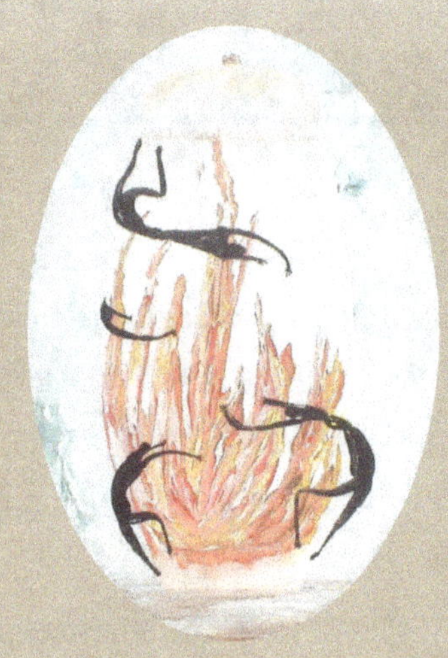

<u>Slowly Conceding</u>
<u>To The Fire</u>

This great world God has given us is slowly
eroding,
and with this loss the people are conforming.

Inch by inch and hour by hour
each of us sink lower and lust power.

If we turn to God and be humble with praise,
He will show us the way and help us to raise,

children who will not conform
but instead will transform.

Changing this carnal population
to a world of adulation.

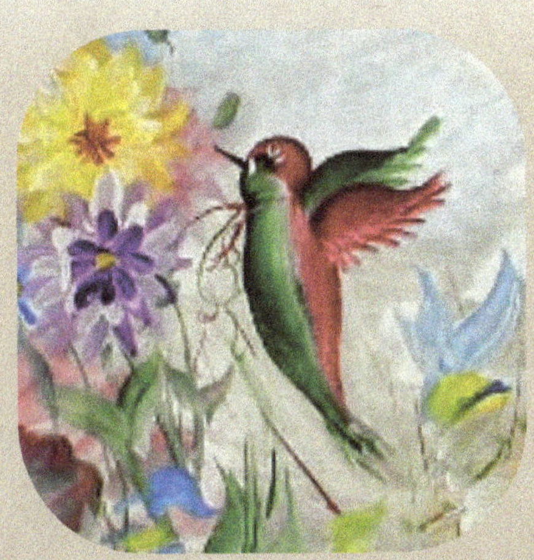

The Glory Of God's Creations

Pretty little birds flit from flower to flower
      up in the air and away from the cats.
Spending their time hour after hour
    seeking their food along well trod paths.

People walk those trails knowing full well
 God placed these beautiful birds so man can know
that on this popular path they'll get their fill
   of which of God's beauty He cares to show.

Blest we are that he wants to share
     with we the chosen free renters of earth;
these fascinating creatures, masters of the air.
    That make us realize He values our worth.

Thank you God; and our Lord, Jesus Christ
 Who; for our salvation paid the ultimate price.

<u>Grief</u>

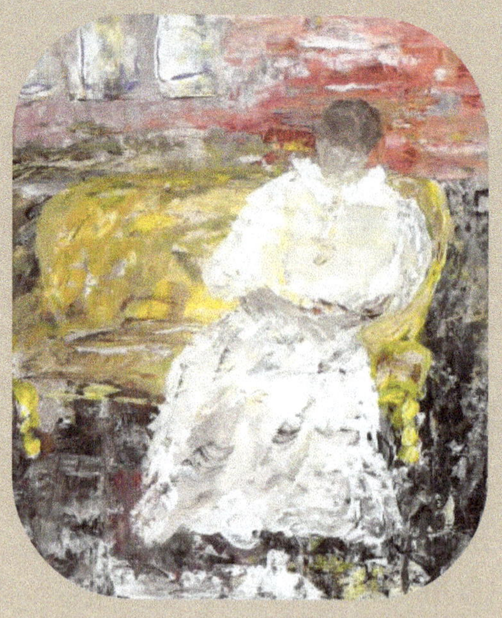

Lovely lady all alone.
Lost her life's chaperone.
Now protected in God's zone.
He watches her from His throne.
Born in Christ with a strong backbone.
She prays every day just to atone;
for the rare random millstone
wrapped around her person,
for which she does moan.

Lovely Lady On A Hill

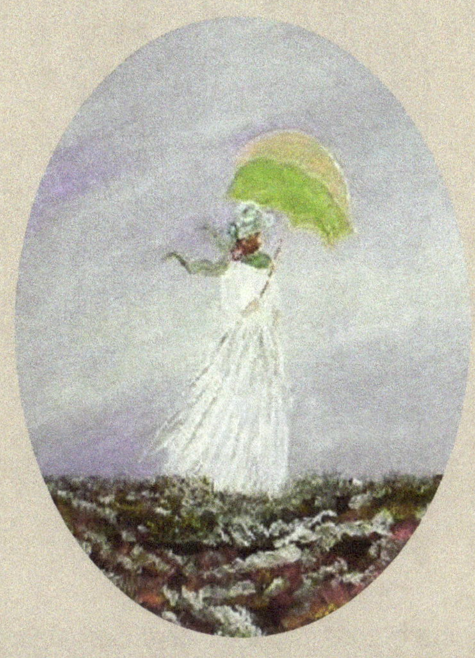

Lonely lovely lady with hair so long and fine.
Do you stand on that hill just to think and pine?
Is it the loss of a loved one
that brings you to tears?
Or perhaps the thought of all those lost years.
Reflect again on a glorious up-bringing
and how you rejoiced in your choir singing.
Then thank the Lord for His Son on the cross
that brought your salvation at His cost.

Dotted Flower

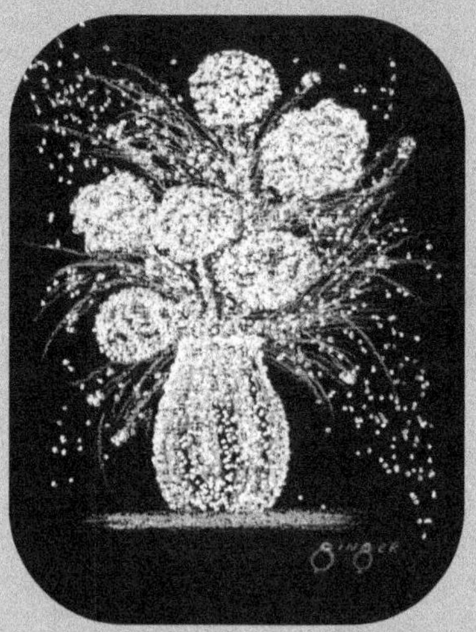

As I stand in my kitchen
looking at the window sill,
I see my dotted flower.
Perfect and still.

A breeze blows through the curtains and
there's a little stir.
I see my dotted flower
perk up and purr.

It makes me happy,
that little dotted flower.
I look at it and
feel strength and power.

That little dotted flower
has an energy all its own.
And it's my great fortune that
the energy is on loan.

For me He created the dotted flower
with His own hand,
and now I'd like to share it
with everyone in the land.

Solid As A Rock

The metaphor of a rock is not unknown.
We use it to threaten,
we use it to atone.

We liken our life to its solidity,
and compare our love
to its validity.

Like working the rock pile
compares our very hard day.
And our good neighbor is
just a stone's throw away.

But the beauty of a rock in the garden
or on the shore
is in the way we have faith
our souls can be ever-more.

As the rock exists beyond our earth life,
we are assure of Heaven
beyond our strife.

I Hear Him Knocking At My Door

I hear Him knocking on my door.
Tap, tap, tapping softly but more and more.
Everywhere I hear his voice or see his face,
cooing, whispering, tempting grace.
"Don't you wish you had his riches."
Or; "You can live like those oil prince's.
Be brave and take a chance.
You can win it all on that dance."

Satan loves to take you down
and make you think you've won the round.
When all along you sink deeper,
descending closer to your fear.
He loves to lure you to the sin,
then laugh as it sucks you in.

Don't fall for his wily ways
that make you think you rule your days.
Look only to Jesus for salvation.
Through Him you can fight temptation.
Ask God to give you life peace.
He will help you fight the Satan beast.

<u>Reflect The Love Of Jesus</u>
<u>In All You Do</u>

I cock my ear to hear what you say and then
wonder if that's what you mean.
Maybe I didn't hear you correctly and I just had
an over-dose of caffeine.
I know my looks don't elicit compliments or
words of adoration.
But if beauty is in the eye of the beholder,
perhaps I could hope for accreditation.
Next time you say such bad things about
someone who is a friend.
Don't forget that that is the way friendships
come to and end.
I'm well aware of who I am and I don't resent
other peoples opinion .
But I live in the grace of Jesus and treat others
with some admiration
as I think He would want us to, with love,
respect and communication.

Loving People

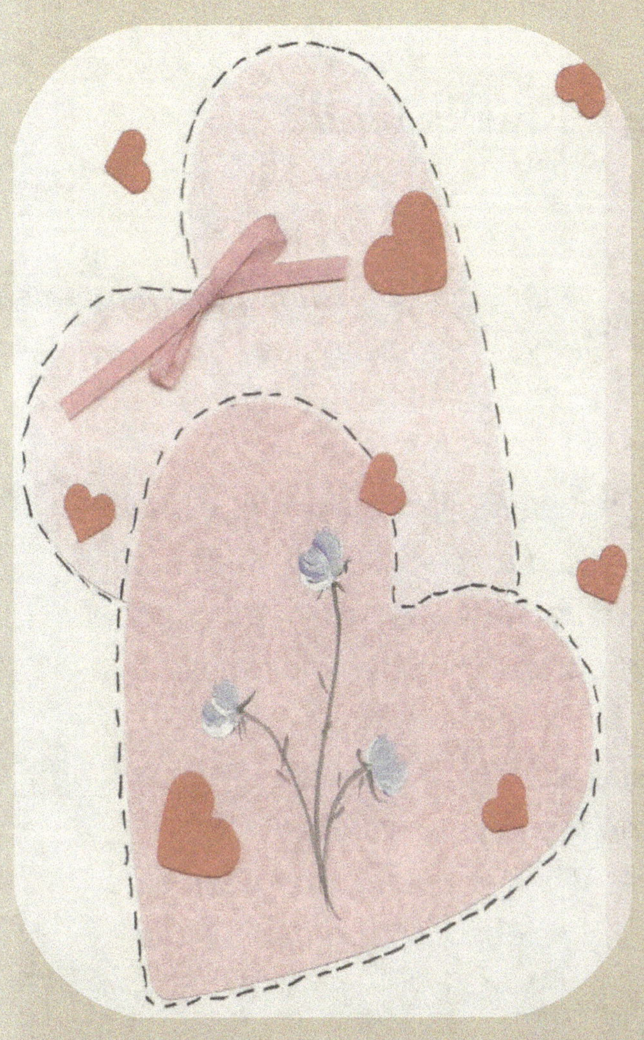

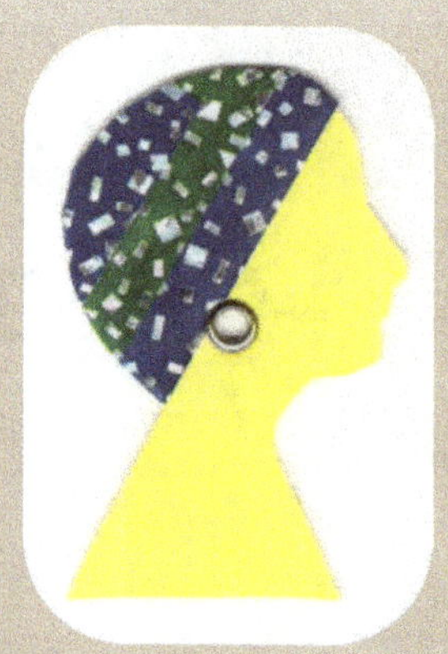

<u>Scary Aunt Gladys</u>

Never one to compromise or bend to anothers will;
aunt Gladys could stiffen her back,
and give those looks that could kill.

I often wondered if she ever kept track
of the kids she scared out of their wits.
Or if she cared how they wished her gone,
or how she got out of her snits.

But then she would put you to bed with a song
and make your world all right.
That was when you knew you were safe,
and could sleep all through the night.

The Sittin And Spittin Spot
Of
My Son Josh And Me

*Close to the road into the woods
where we'd talk of fools and hoods,
watch for crickets and listen to cars;
was a place that we simply called ours.*

*Talking manly things tween father and son,
planning the future and fishing for fun,
aptly describes this tree dimmed plot.
One that will always be my favorite spot.*

That's Josh and my sittin and spittin spot.

*The years pass by but there time waits
for memories of closeness never a waste.
Closeness between generations found
wisdom passed both up and down.*

*Lessons I learned from a young thinking lad
brightened the old cobby thoughts I had.
Formed a bond never broken or pulled taut,
and laid groundwork for generations yet thought.*

At Josh and my sittin and spittin spot.

*Whether or not he returns to it,
he knows the import of a place to sit
with his son and learn the joy of
spending time with his own boy.
They'll be together and talk and whittle.
Dab some stones and maybe fish a little.
Listen to each other's hopes and joys.
Maybe mention grandpa and just be boys.*

Like Josh and My Sittin and Spitten Spot.

<u>Happy 50th Anniversary</u>

You started so young and worked thru blood,
sweat and tears,
but that made your love strong
through the years.

A life built together that
none could put asunder.
Through ups and downs and
the occasional blunder.

But through it all, you've
accomplished much
And there's still that thrill
when you touch.

But there's another reason
you're still together
You've got fifty more to weather.

You'll continue to love and accomplish much.
But this time there is no rush!

You'll take it slower and enjoy life more,
and be together in heaven when this is oer.

The Heart Of The Bride's Mother

With eye of tears and heart of pride
this major step one must take in stride.

To conquer the apprehension of the unknown
and look forward to this move to being full grown,
brings rushing back all the ups and downs
of guidance through love with anguish and frowns.

How can this gift of my loins through God
be successful without my occasional prod?

But sure in my teachings and my child's reliance
to walk with Jesus and trust in His guidance,
I am secure in the knowledge she will get through
continuing her journey knowing I'm true.

My heart is filled with confidence, love and faith,
As I know she can conquer all she will face.

<u>Tribute To My Friend TC</u>

Soaring over the fog shrouded hills
We think of our beloved one's pains and ills
That are now relieved by God's ethereal skills.

The strength and joy he generously instilled
gave hope and direction to those so willed
to learn from him, and in life become skilled.

To become adept with life's alterations
learning to steer from all stations,
and how to set one's own expectations.

Although he will be sorely missed,
his print on our lives will forever exist.
In family and friends his memory will persist.

Aiden's Lucky Birth

Sometimes I can't believe my luck
the way God put me on this earth.
I thought He considered me a schmuck
and just gave me a random birth.

Then I met this beautiful blond.
She cared for me and fed me good
and told me she's my mom,
and would always be there as she should.

Besides that; to make things even better,
there's this other girl around the place.
Beautiful and perfect to the letter
and seems to have a lot of grace.

At first I thought she was the sitter
But nah --- seems she just my sister.

A Tribute To My Great Granddaughter

The beauty of a woman is more than her shape.
It's what's in her head and her heart we appreciate.

A fine tuned body shows she is aware of her health.
With a sharp and quick mind she can amass wealth.

But what really stands out and sets her apart,
is the kindness and generosity in her heart.

Your beauty is what people first see of you,
and the power of your brain will carry you through.

*But your connection to God
is through your heart,
and
that is what sets
your strong character apart.*

Amira, My Grandniece

Once upon a time
a beautiful princess turned nine,
and said,
"due to my parents I'll be fine".
She looked in the mirror
and called herself Amira.
This prettiest little princess of an era.

They'll know when she's fooling,
and will look after her schooling,
all the while teaching her to be kind.
This pretty little princess turned nine.

They will praise her ways when she does good,
and direct her path as all parents should.
And then pull her away
when she's headed astray.
This pretty little princess
who will learn the way.

She's pert and pretty and smart as a whip,
and can talk your ears off at a pretty good clip.
She dances and draws as good as the best.
This pretty little princess beats all the rest.

Enjoy being nine and learn all you can.
Don't fret your future you'll outsmart any man.
Always love your mom and dad and your brother too.
Love God and be good He will take care of you.

<u>The Power Of Prayer</u>

God gave us a baby to show us the joy
of raising a child, whether it be girl or boy.

But little did we know the strength we would find
when her sister was born with a problem unkind.

Hanna was born with a life-threatening defect,
and Callie showed us how faith summons reject.

Through the power of prayer and unwavering love,
we marched through hard times
with help from above.

Now Hannah has parents, family and a sister too,
to share her life, her love and to see her through.

The Birth Of
Grandnephew Junaid

Whether dropped from the sky as a bundle of joy,
or brought by a stork from some distant shore.
The birth of a child now known to be a boy
was worth the morning sickness and everything more.

Delighted with a daughter, so pretty and bright
a son would add a whole new panorama,
to a life filled with hope, joy and insight.
A broadened view of an already wide drama.

To take on the responsibility of filling his
mind, body and soul is daunting in thought.
But the hope of perfection upon completion
overwhelms the fears bringing them to naught.

Thank you God, and bide with us.
Your divine guidance and aid,
in this great task You have set upon us,
help and be with us as we raise Junaid.

Sisterly Love

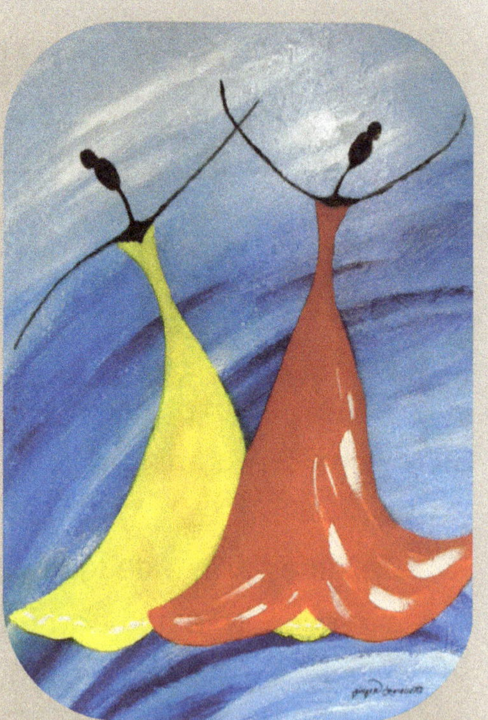

I was watching
two little girls
at the market one day,
and
I could tell they were
sisters
by the way
they would play.

The older one; who was quite a bit bigger,
would play kind of rough, but then she would hug her.

Although they were young; both early grade,
I knew they were building what would never fade.

I could see in the future that squabbles would occur.
But they had built a foundation
that would forever endure.

Then; in their later years as they age and wither,
They both know the closeness that they did nurture.

So, when God comes for one and they are finally apart.
The one that is gone, lives on in the others heart.

<u>The Union Of Oneness</u>

Your beauty fills the air:
clean and pure and everywhere.
Close; so near I touch your ear, your tongue
and nose.
You touched me, and I froze.
Sounds of peace between us cease ,
and passion pushes peace aside
and reasons hide.
Heat and fire fill the room our bodies flow, fly
and carom.
Peace returns, bodies part, souls united,
linked by heart.
Your beauty fills the air,
clean and pure and everywhere.

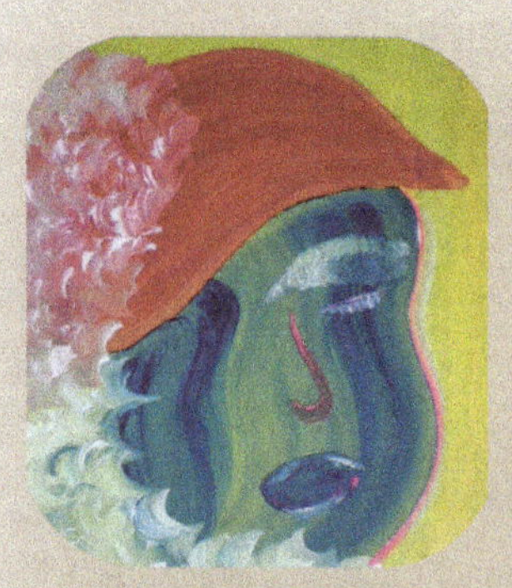

<u>Beauty Is In The Beholder</u>

*(Fortunately: God has blessed some people
with the empathy to see the inner beauty
of the person they are attracted to.)*

My lady treats me good. I see the beauty inside.
You guys don't understand and ask
what I'm trying to hide.

She's been called a dog, cucumber nose and
more.
But she loves me every day, and warms me to
my core.

What is really nice about your blindness,
is that you leave her alone. I thank you for your
kindness.

<u>Just Off the Trail</u>

Just a step or two off the trail and
into the woods a ways,
there's a place that's perfect for us
to laze away the days.
Flowers that bloom, a bubbling creek with a fish or two.
Peace and quiet and beauty. Just the place to renew.
I like to think of it as my private rendezvous.
That private place to spend time with you.
The whiz and blur of the day is past
and we are together at last.
No longer apart, then I
remember "you are
ever in my heart"

Transition To Adulthood

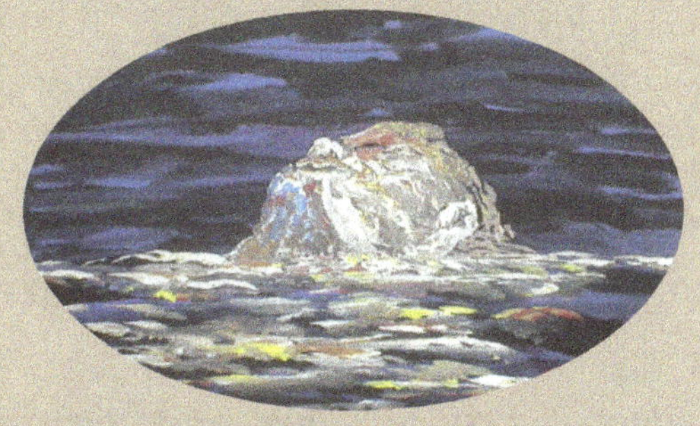

Rising from the water with our face toward the sky.
As though from a deep sleep, we rise asking why.

What is this new horizon and what will be asked of me?
Will my existence go to slave from one of liberty?

The transition from known to unknown
shakes one's confidence nigh unto the bone.

But transcend we must in order to grow.
And become a responsible adult in the know.

And avoid the pitfalls of neglect and irresponsibility
that has ruined the lives of so many of possibility.

Let our mother show the way. She knows
right from wrong.
She has the strength to uplift us
and her love is very strong.

Look to her for guidance she will show us the way.
She is our inspiration and motivation everyday.

No Mountain Too Tall

Each loss in our lives is a milestone for reflection.
Every lesson learned and from which direction.

If you recall your school years and some hard nosed teachers,
you can see how some lessons were filled
with scary features.

And tough though they were and demanding of you,
you look back with love and know that's how you grew.

At this milestone of loss you know you can look
ahead, and handle the coming challenges without dread.

Because your strong character and God's hand
guided you through tough times and harsh land.

You still have that strength and good friends too,
and God is always there still guiding you.

Whimsical

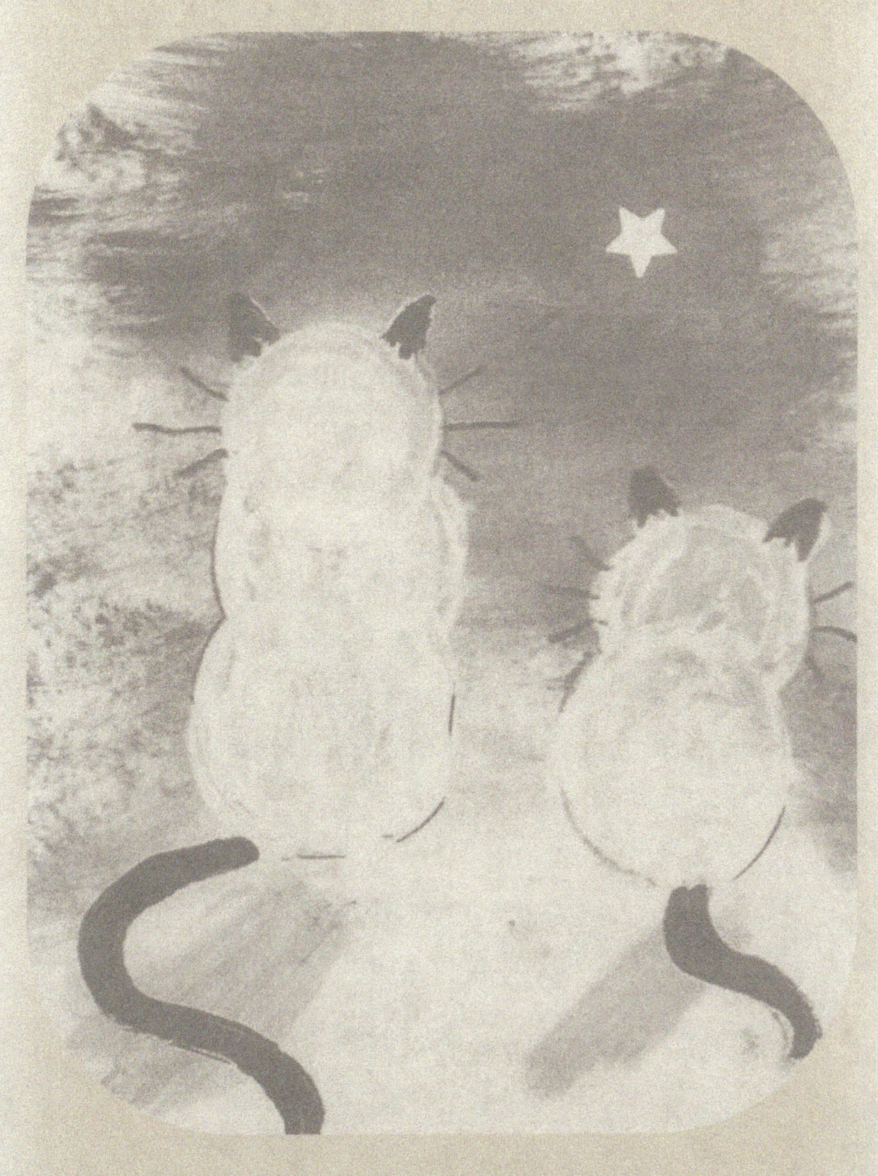

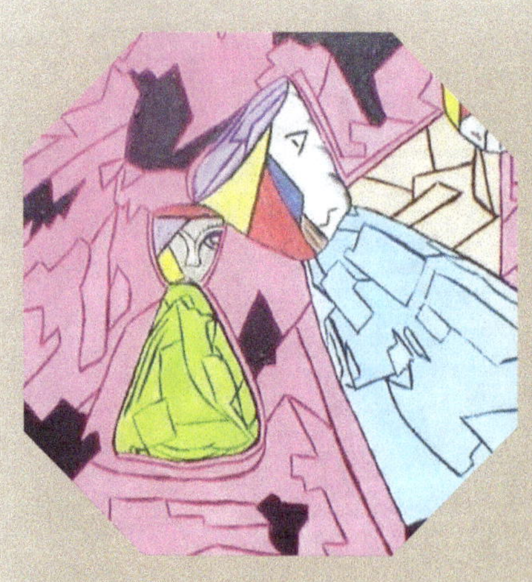

<u>This</u>
<u>Crazy World</u>

Isn't this a crazy world with people rock'n round.

Silly meander'n to and fro with no direction found.

Best be think'n how yer mov'n and

to where yer bound.

Or you'll be naught but chessmen

not a one that's sound.

Grieves me though it does and

singe's my eye brows.

Sometimes me thinks that man is as silly as

two legged cows.

Wanting nothing more to do than to tell

stories and carouse.

Settle back in the recliner and

store away the plows.

Cozy Cozy Cozy

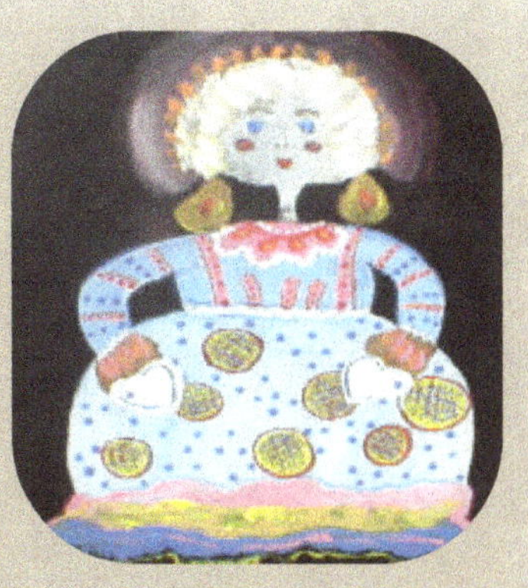

She looks so pretty with painted face,
Rosy cheeks and full of grace.
Cozy look like Mama had.
Especially when she looked at Dad.
I'm sure she's warm as a bird roaster.
Of course she is.
She's sitting on a toaster.

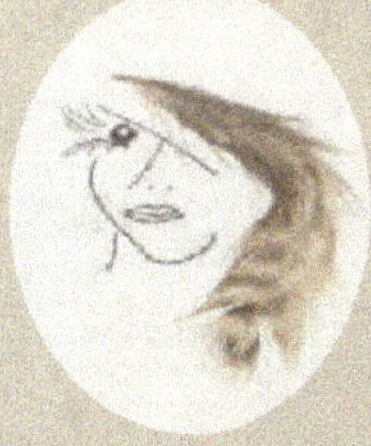

She's The One

If a lady wants to look mysterious and demure,
all she need do is cover an eye and look secure.

Take a large feather, preferably one that is rare.
Then look from behind it showing "I don't care".

Whether she's pretty or not, or even rich or poor,
she'll make you believe she's the one.
There are no more.

<u>Some Pets Are Life Savers</u>

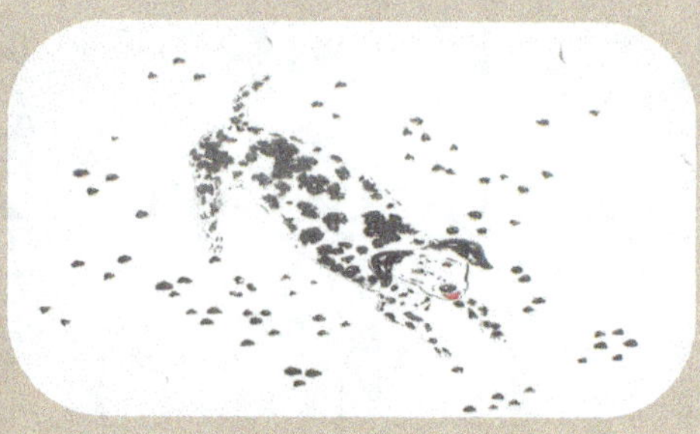

I don't want you to think I'm silly,
or that I'd make an outrageous demand.
Trust me, I don't worry if I get chilly,
but I am a very important brand.

My breed is known for ultimate valor,
and it's important we're found in the field.
But I carry for identity more than my color.
The spots on my body are my shield.

So it's important to me that I keep my
identity,
and the firemen know where I am.

So why they come off every time I shake,
is a really scary mistake.

Cat Games

I thought I saw a puddy tat a lookin up at me,
and everywhere I'd try to hide he still could look at me.
I hurried here and hurried there and finally said to self,
the only safe place I can find is up above that shelf.
Safely hidden out of sight and quiet as a mouse,
I waited for him to search the house.
I soon began to see that things weren't quite the same,
then discovered the reason why.
He'd quit playing the game.

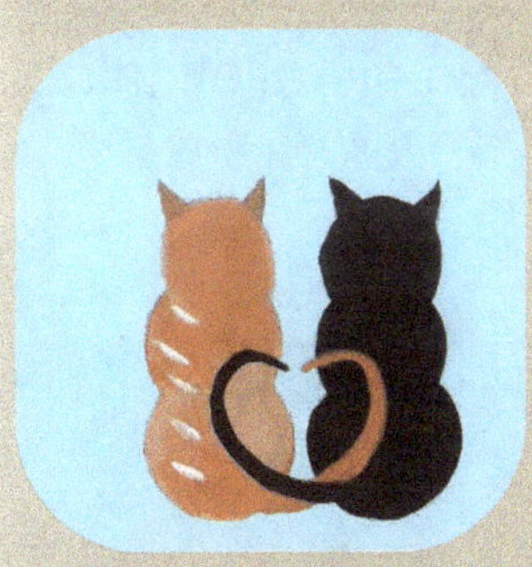

Brothers In The Hood

Brothers in the hood. Some
bad some good.
Running through the alleys
looking for some food.
Time to stop and chat a while.
Looking for something to
defile.
Isn't it great to have such a
friend.
One that will see you through
to the end.

Skinny Cat

Skinny cat sittin on the ground.
Spun his head lookin around.
Blinked his eyes and lost his face.
Wondered then who took his place.
He's sittin outside instead of in his house.
Rather be inside lookin for a mouse.
Whoever put him out didn't understand.
He only tore it up cause it smelt to beat the band.
If they are going to treat him mean,
He'll just stay out and do his alley thing.

Ode To The Master Of The House

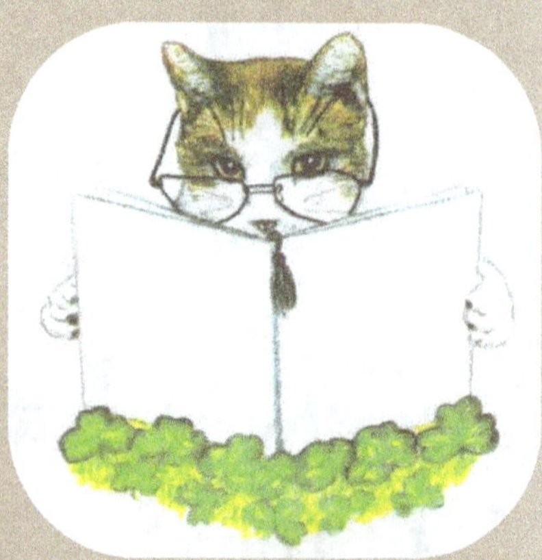

Known to be smart
as a breed,
this pretty lady
knows your need.
She'll curl round your leg,
almost as to beg.
Then, as you trip,
run off with great speed.

Where Is Her Heart

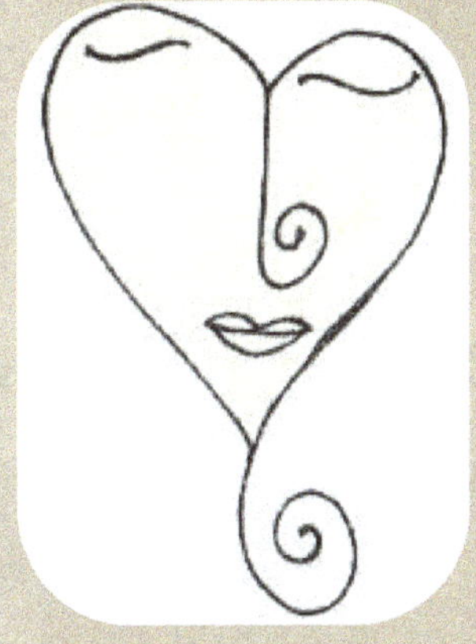

There was this pretty young tart.
Who tried to hide her heart.
But would you believe,
instead of her sleeve,
her face was shaped like a heart.

Smart Blonde

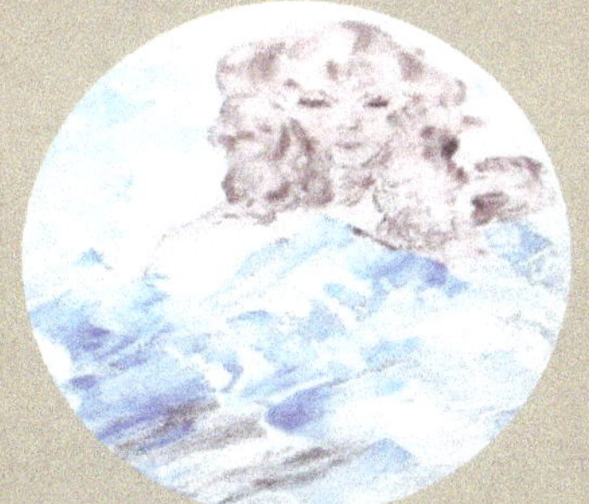

Who ever said that blonds are dumb knows
not of what they speak.
Just watch this beauty do her thing and
never miss a beat.
She'll bum some drinks and a dinner too
and promise a good time soon.
But when she's done and had her fill she'll
up and leave the room.

Living The Life

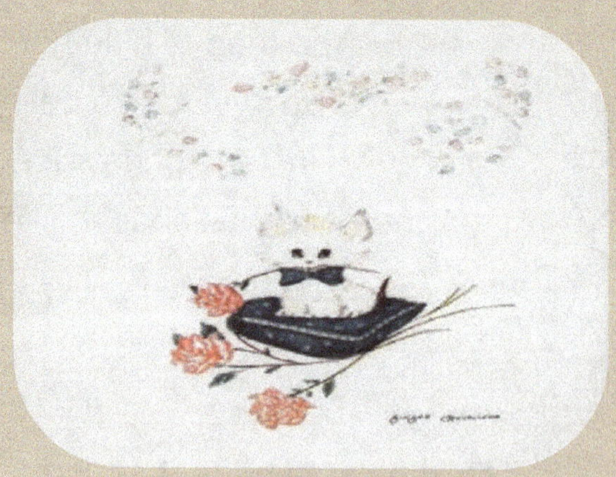

Cuddly little kitten drenched in luxury.
Say goodbye to hunger, woe and misery.
Thank the lady at the pound
who took the time to show you 'round'.
Then turn three times and curl on your
pillow.
Thank those folks and the SPCA fellow.
And prepare to instruct the new winners
on how you expect your dinners.

Half-Headed Wisdom

I wouldn't exactly say I am a genius,
But I've found the cure
for what is mean to us.

When you start to get
half a head-ache,
vanish that half, then wait.

Your friends might think
you look a bit weird
but it's not as bad
as you feared.

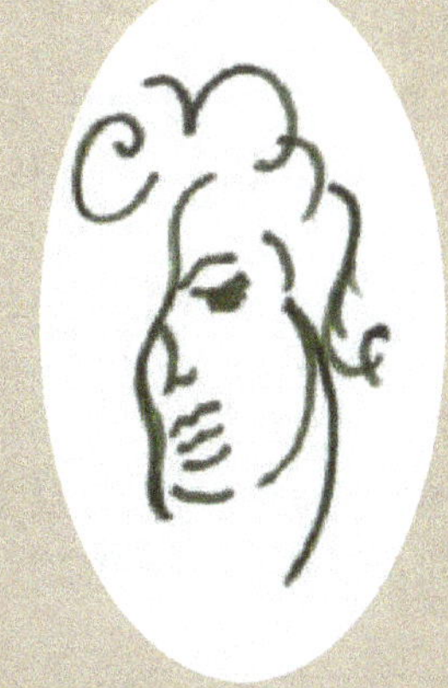

You keep your hair and good looks too.
Besides, they are as weird as you.

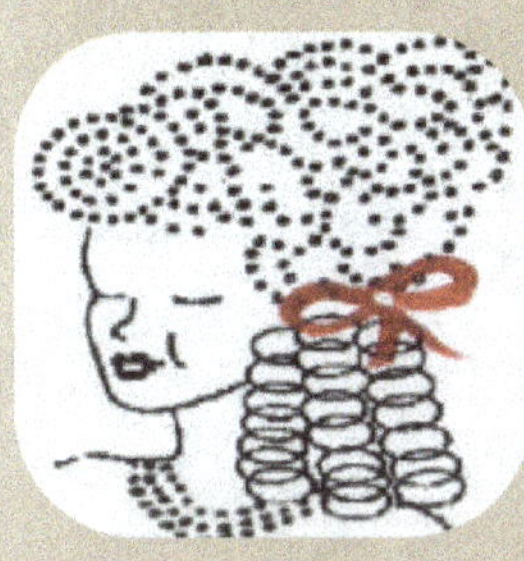

The Aristocrat

Lady of grace with curls so high
properly dressed and narrow of eye.

Think you are so proper of judgment
and make your opinions abundant.

Pretty of face and fashionably poofed
but squinty eyed and very aloof.

Don't bring your Victorian hypocrisy
and act like you're of aristocracy.

Caribbean Island Bongo Drummer

Thump-a-thump thump on my bongos I drum.
I love to do it, it's a lot of fun.

Hop here, hop there and shake a little booty,
my mommy thinks I'm a real cutie.

Make yourself a hat and a skirt from a leaf.
Got to keep your costume real brief.

Gives you more room to shuffle your feet.
And gets you loose to keep up the beat.

<u>Inside Silicon Valley</u>

*Once upon a time I wished that I could see
right through a man and into his mind,
and learn what makes him be he.
I don't know what I'd look for or
what it is I'd find.*

*But I'd like to know if he's thinking
about money, power and fame,
or whether he's been drinking
and just didn't see things the same.*

*Then I saw a man at a computer.
I looked at him and hoped to pray
that I could see his minds future.
I stared and stared and pretended to x-ray.*

*Then it opened up so I could see his mind.
But as deep as I could look there was only a
computer sign.*

Holiday Tributes

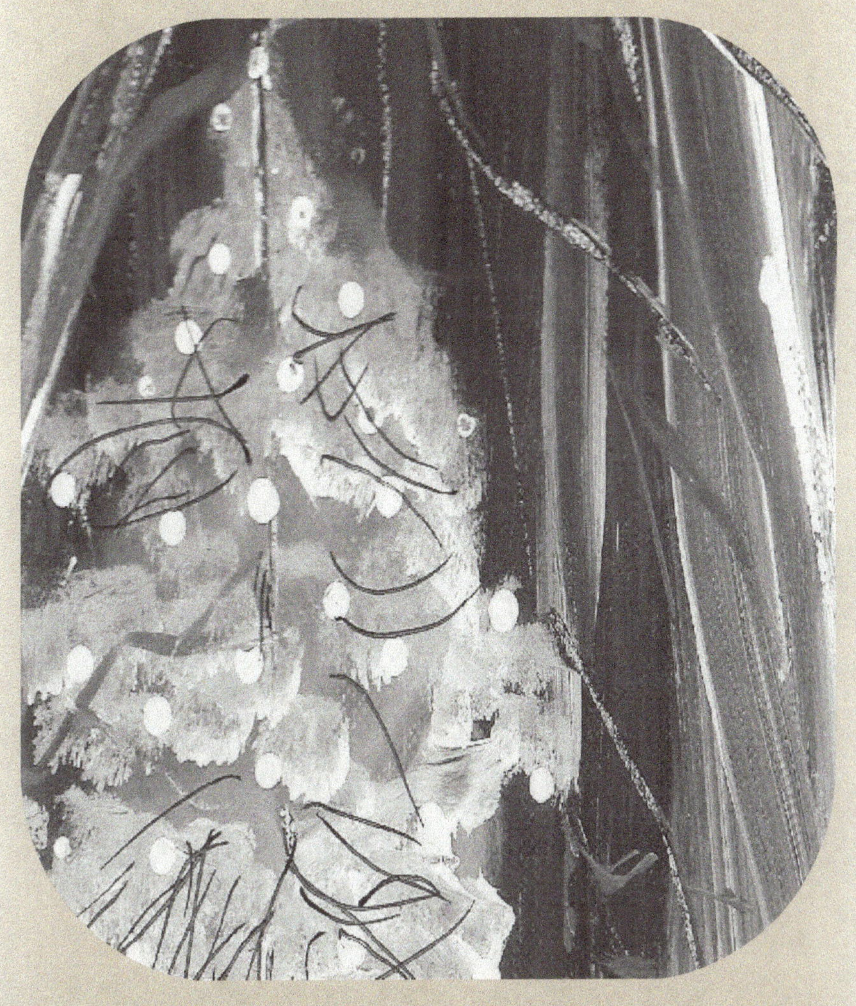

<u>Halloween Lyrics</u>

Twas dark and late on a cold and dreary night;
And I was at a loss, deep in thought and weary a mite.

With out a care of way or route, I came upon a scary sight.
A headless man and three zombies were jumping around
as in a fight.

Then someone hollered trick or treat and
I knew it was alright.
This is that special time of witches, it's Halloween night.

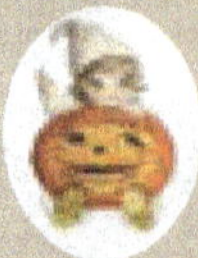

*That crazy old lady up the street
ugly as sin with great big feet.*

*Big ugly nose topped by a hairy wart.
Long grayish hair, she's the real witchy sort.*

*When she chortles and cracks a grin,
You see a big gaping hole from nose to chin.*

*What's really scary and most obscene.
She's that way when it isn't even halloween.*

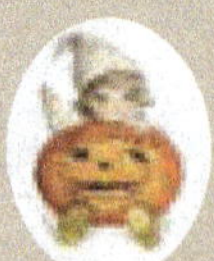

I hear the pitter-patter of their feet,

a sneakin up from off the street.

One by one they creep to the door.

They leap and jump for candy and more.

I love to watch their tricks and give the treat.

Then listen as they scamper down the street.

Who says Halloween is just for children.

That's one night I can feel cool again.

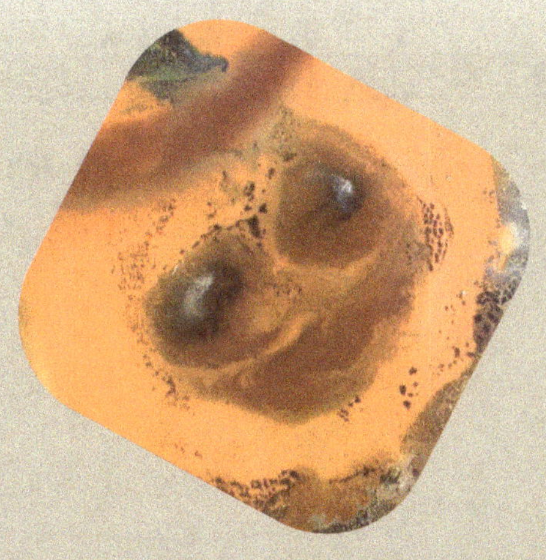

The Joy Of Being A Pumpkin

Halloween pumpkins take a bad rap.
You carve us up scary, or funny and fat.

Then light a candle in our innards.
Hoping people will think we are wizards.

There's nothing magic about a pumpkin.
But the way we're treated is discourg'in

I keep thinking about my cousin;
He was cooked in a pie and got lots'o lovin.

The Christmas Tree
Of Timmy Terrible

I
spy
a dry
wee eye
crying over
Christmas eve.
Thought our Santa
wouldn't dare deceive
some who did not believe.
But caught there under a glow
with no pretty toy or a gift to show
was Mr.
"I know
I'm too
bad to
grow."

Celebrate The Birth Of Christ

I love the reason for the season,
But hate the way we celebrate.

We make a mockery of the birth
and turn the season into one of mirth.

God gave us His Son for our salvation.
Not to celebrate with recreation.

Every day should be a day to commemorate.
One on which we can exhilarate.

So hereafter I shall worship every day
as Christmas in every way.

God's Gift

God has blessed us with many gifts.
Now we celebrate His greatest gift of all.
He gave His only begotten Son
So that we should not fall.

Let us begin the New Year in Harmony.
With love and peace everywhere.
Blessing friends and family
With very special care.

Walk With Christ

God gave us life and freedom of goals
then gave us His son to redeem our souls.
We can choose our path and the way we trod
but Jesus died so we can be with God.

Now is the time to celebrate the birth
that brought us this gift of our life's worth.
Because we cherish His life and this gift
we'll not lower ourselves to be politically fit.

But wish a Merry Christ-mas to you and yours
instead of Holiday Greeting
and meaningless cheers.

May your entire life be a walk with Christ.

Christmas Friends

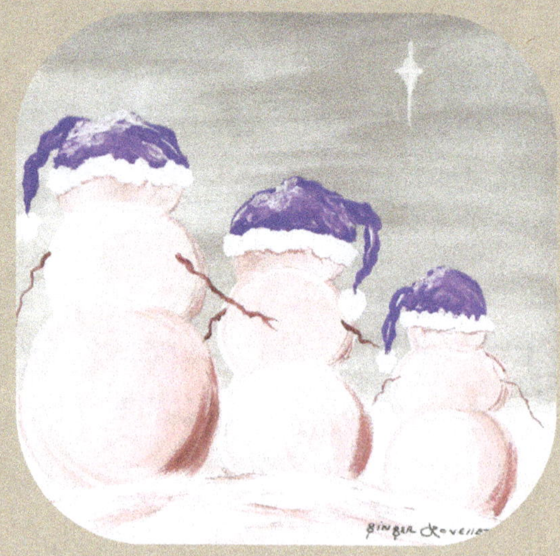

With Christmas around the corner
our thoughts go out to friends.

Makes us wonder why the heck
we wait until each year ends.
.
While Christ is in our hearts year-long
shouldn't our friends be along.

It seems to us they really are there
but we forget somehow just where.

Thank God for giving us Christ and you,
and thank God for friends and family too.

Happy Valentine

This is the day, just the right time
to express your love to your valentine.

Do more than talk to show how you feel
and explain to her what is her appeal.

Shower her with gifts and candy
and adding some roses would be just dandy.

But without sincerity all is lost
and out the door you will be tossed.

Rejoice The Birth

62

This mysterious and marvelous world we live in
is a gift from God and was freely given.

What He wants from us is righteous living
and a return of His love as thanks giving.

He set some laws that would help our behavior.
Then Satan stepped in and became an enabler.

To grant us redemption God sent us His Savior
to teach us love and Christian behavior.

Let us now celebrate the birth of His Son
and give thanks for the salvation offered to everyone.

Halloween Scare

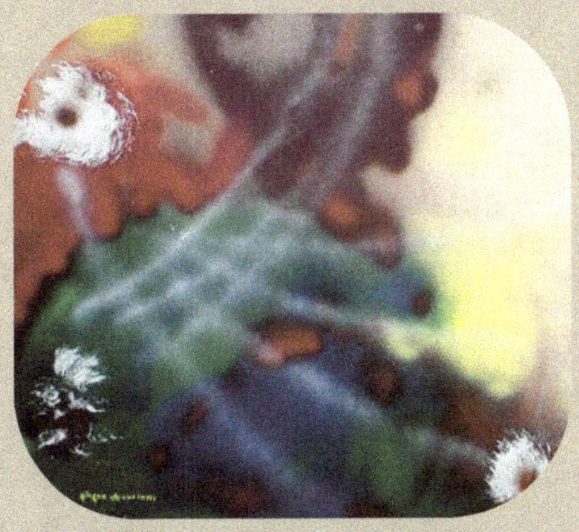

If you think the big bad wolf is scary,
listen to a story that's really hairy.
One dark and dreary, chilly night.
I was walking down an alley out of sight.
Minding my own business but snooping just a bit
When all of a sudden, out of nowhere I was hit.
There was screaming and shouting from off somewhere
My only thought was to get the heck out of there.
I ran as fast as I could, out away from that awful scare
And that's when I noticed there were people everywhere.
Dancing in the street, jumping up and down.
Then I looked and saw a big fat clown.
He came directly at me pushing folks away
I knew that this was going to be my payday.
That retribution for all of the bad I had done.
He was going to push my final button.
That's when I heard my awful scream
and I awoke from that frightful dream.
HAPPY HALLOWEEN

Night Of The Weird

Fiery demons dancing around,
big nosed clowns falling down.
I see satan showing off a crown.
A funny old man wearing a gown.
What in the world's happening in town?
Is the world falling apart or being torn down?
Must be witching night countdown
because weirdness seems to abound.

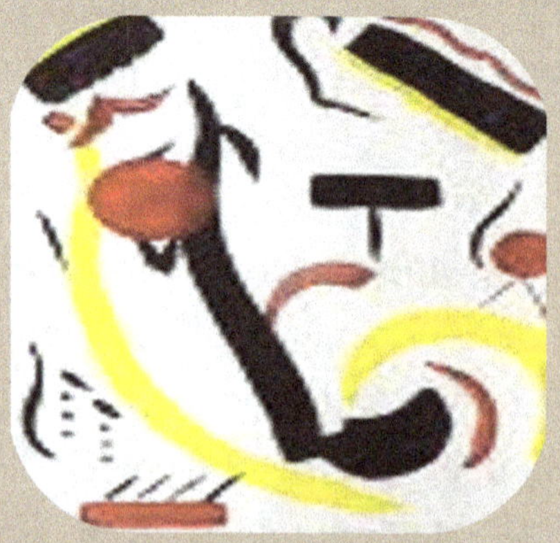

Trickin For Candy

Ever wonder if those ghost are real
and goblins are something you can feel.
I wonder if demons are really there,
and not imagined just to scare.
When it's dark and eerie at night
and I see things that just aren't right.
I ask myself about trickin n treatin,
is it worth the candy from whom your meetin.
About that time when I'm scared to be seen,
is when it becomes fun on Halloween.

Hickory, Dickory, Plop

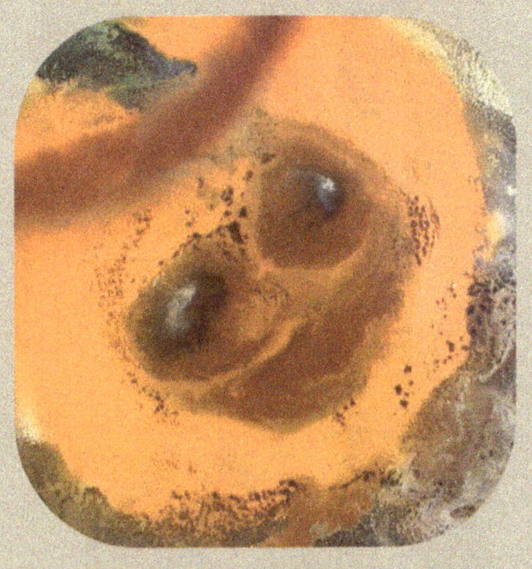

Hickory, dickory, plop.
A pumpkin fell off the dock.

He soon was picked up
by a kid in a truck,

and was carted away
for surgery that day.

But when he came to
he knew he was through.

Cause his smile was simpy
and his head was empty.

Holy Birth

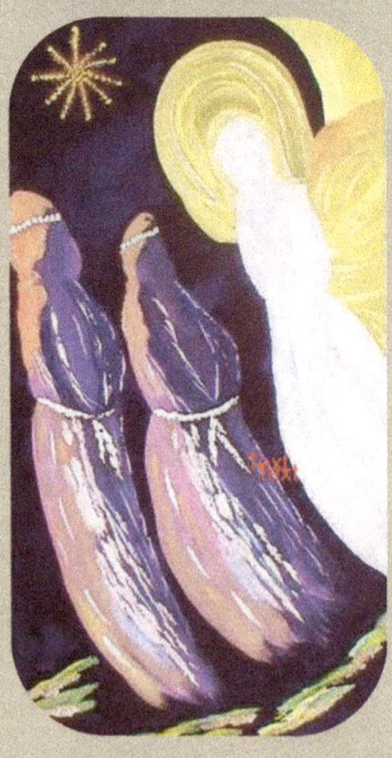

As the shepherds were tending their flock at night;

an angel approached them, it was quite a sight.

To think God would select them to bring the news

of the birth of His son and the King of the Jews.

They fell to their knees in awe and reverent fear.

But knew they were blest to know salvation was near.

They knew that all the world would soon hear

how much God loved them and they needn't fear.

His new born Son lay in a manger not far away.

And they would tell of this moment

to their final day.

The Warmth Of God's Love

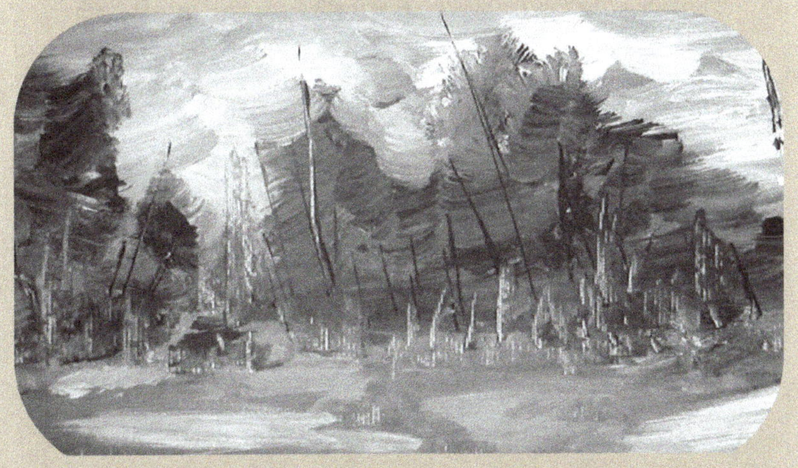

What greater warmth
on a snowy cold night
than knowing Jesus came
to make things right.

A God so loving
to give such a gift
as His very own Son
to heal every rift.

No greater love
could man behold
than that,
as God has bestowed.

Now is the time
to praise His birth
and celebrate
His time on earth.

So love each other
and live in kindness
And thank God
for His gift of Christmas.

The Birth Of A Special Boy

Foretold by ancient prophets of old.
The coming of our Savior was often told.

Sent to this earth for our salvation.
He was mostly greeted with blind rejection.

Sadly, today it's not much different.
There are those who remain belligerent.

So during these days as we celebrate His birth;
let us pray for those who know not their worth.

So that they may fully know the real joy
of celebrating the birth of this very special Boy.

The Troubled Christmas Of 2021

Oh Jesus; brightest star of Bethlehem,
your light shines on a world in bedlam.
Absorbed in greed and lust for power
You see us not at our best hour.

As we all gather to honor your birth
we thank Your Father for His gift to earth.
His great love reflected by You
taught us the joy of love in all we do.

We wish that same love
to our friends and family.
May this Christmas
be one of joy and amenity.
And His love be reflected
on you and yours
throughout tomorrow and
the remaining years.

We Praise A Loving God

Once upon a shining star
God guided Magi from afar.

Destined to honor the birth of a King.
They found the Savior of all being.

Only a loving God would bestow grace
Upon such an unthankful race.

But a loving God knows the demons we fight
And through His Son, offers heaven's light.

On bended knee we praise His birth
And honor His message as He walked this earth.